# Contents

Teach us, Lord

Why small groups?

In St Luke's account of the Early Church we hear that three thousand were baptised following Pentecost (Acts 2:41). Guided by the Holy Spirit, the newly baptised 'devoted themselves to the apostles' teaching and fellowship, to the breaking of bread and the prayers' (Acts 2:42). In a similar fashion thousands of people have found spiritual nourishment in faith-sharing, in reflecting on Scripture and prayer as part of a small group.

This resource feeds such small groups drawing on the Scriptures with each session clearly rooted in a passage from the Bible. As the Second Vatican Council Fathers emphasised 'in the sacred books the Father comes lovingly to meet his children and talks with them' (*Dei Verbum*, 21).

Fellowship is a vital part of small group participation. In these small groups you are able to get to know your fellow Christians better and to form strong, mutually supportive bonds. The living community is essentially Christian as Jesus 'did not come to save individuals without any bond between them' (*Lumen Gentium*, 9).

Members of small groups are encourgaed to share and gain confidence in talking about their faith. It is this confidence building in a trusting environment that helps participants to 'love in all the circumstances of ordinary life' (*Gaudium et Spes*, 38). Our prayers together help us to become the dwelling places of the Holy Spirit that we are called to be (*Sacrosanctum Concilium*, 2).

How do small groups work?

The sessions in this booklet are designed to last between 1 and 1 ½ hours. Those leading the session are, of course, free to add periods of silence, hymns and other readings of interest - these sessions are a guide but can be used as they are written.

It is vital that each person is given the opportunity to give their thoughts and share where they are on their faith journey. Small group sharing is not a place for argument or heated debate.

The atmosphere should be prayerful with the aim of helping each to feel welcome and conscious of God's loving presence. Soft music, candlelight, a religious image or crucifix to focus attention can all be used to help in this aim.

# Foreword

Dear brothers and sisters,

It is hard to imagine a more beautiful request than the one made by the disciples when they asked Jesus to teach them how to pray (Luke 11:1). In this simple request they are seeking guidance from their Master, a deeper relationship with their Creator and a closer bond with one another. In response he gave us the gift of the 'Our Father'.

Prayer is central to the life of any believer. Yet its pattern and form is not the same for all. What some find helpful in prayer may leave others unmoved. Throughout our lives we may find that our patterns of prayer change, the way we talk to God alters over time, not least as a result of experience. At different stages of life, indeed even at different times in the same day, we may find moments where prayer is fruitful and occasions when it seems to be empty and dry.

This booklet, which I commend to your attention, is not a practical guide to prayer nor is it a simple prayer book. Instead it is an exploration of the underlying principles of prayer. Through its pages we will come to share our experiences of prayer, drawing on Scripture and the teaching of the Church. We will explore our prayer as an involvement, as a conversation with God whom we love, through good times and bad, in our youth and as we mature.

So much in Scripture, of which this booklet makes frequent use, leads us deeper into prayer. Indeed Pope Emeritus Benedict XVI described the Book of Psalms as the book of prayer 'par excellence'. His successor Pope Francis has encouraged us all to read Psalm 102 every day (*ed. often numbered 103 and entitled 'God is love'*). Through this season, as groups and as individuals, let us take inspiration from the psalmist: Blessing the Lord at all times; with his praise continually on our lips. May our souls make their boast in the Lord as we exalt his name together (Psalm 34:1-2).

Yours devotedly,

+ Vincent Nichols

The Most Reverend Vincent Nichols
Archbishop of Westminster

Teach us, Lord

About this book

'The deeper our faith, the stronger our hope, the greater our desire, the larger will be our capacity to receive the gift, which is very great indeed... The more fervent the desire, the more worthy will be its fruits. When the Apostle tells us: Pray without ceasing (1 Thessalonians 5:16), he means this: Desire unceasingly that life of happiness which is nothing if not eternal, and ask it of him alone who is able to give it.' (St Augustine of Hippo - Letter 130).

Teach us to Pray is the Diocese of Westminster's faith-sharing resource on prayer and has been prepared by the Agency for Evangelisation with the assistance of the Home Mission Desk at the Bishops' Conference.

Teach us to Pray is divided into six group sessions which explore the nature of prayer through life, using William Shakespeare's 'seven ages of man' as a structure. Session One refers to the **Little Ones** and our prayer for the newborn and unborn; Session Two then looks at how we learn to pray in **Childhood**. Session Three explores **Youth** and prayer as a conversation in love and is followed by Session Four which shows us as we **Mature in our Faith**, looking to make a mark on the world. Session Five considers the **Wisdom** of middle age and Session Six looks at the lives of the elderly in terms of joy and humility as we become **Close to the Father.**

In addition to the Scripture and reflections now familiar to users of *exploring faith* booklets, you will find a sprinkling of text boxes explaining various terms. The Scripture passages have been chosen to reflect the theme of their respective sessions and you will benefit from reading the passage in context (that is, reading the passages before and after the one chosen) either as a group or individually.

The booklet is illustrated with a selection of pictures and looking upon these images may stir a thought or feeling in a way that the text could not. We also invite you to make use of the materials in the second part of the booklet which include daily prayers drawn from the Divine Office.

Teach us to Pray is not tied to a particular time of year and the prayers and meditations may be used by individuals, groups or in a wider parish context throughout the year. Additional reflections and thoughts can be found on our small group blog - *a threefold cord is not easily broken* [http://dowsmallgroups. wordpress.com]. This booklet and others in the *exploring faith* series can be viewed at and downloaded from the Diocese of Westminster's website. [http:// rcdow.org.uk/faith/small-groups/resources/]

Teach us, Lord

1. The Little Ones

All the world's a stage, and all the men and women merely players; they have their exits and their entrances, and one man in his time plays many parts, His acts being seven ages. At first, the infant, mewling and puking in the nurse's arms. William Shakespeare, As You Like It

In this first session of *Teach us to Pray* we will reflect on the early stages of life as a time of unfulfilled potential. As the little ones grow, parents and the wider community pray for the child's happiness and help to develop its personal relationship with God.

Image: The Virgin and Child enthroned by Duccio di Buoninsegna (1308-1311)

Teach us, **Lord**

The Little Ones

Opening Prayers
Taken from Psalm 104(103) - to be said all together or the group can divide in half and alternate

All: In the name of the Father, and of the Son, and of the Holy Spirit. Amen.

A: Bless the Lord, my soul!
Lord God, how great you are,
clothed in majesty and glory,
wrapped in light as in a robe!

B: How many are your works, O Lord!
In wisdom you have made them all.
The earth is full of your riches.

A: You hide your face, they are dismayed;
you take back your spirit, they die,
returning to the dust from which they came.

B: You send forth your spirit, they are created;
and you renew the face of the earth.

A: May the glory of the Lord last for ever!
May the Lord rejoice in his works!

B: May my thoughts be pleasing to him.
I find my joy in the Lord.

All: Glory be to the Father, and to the Son and to the Holy Spirit. As it was in the beginning, is now, and ever shall be, world without end. Amen.

As we come together let us, either aloud or in the silence of our hearts, give thanks and praise to the Lord for all the things we have accomplished, the joys experienced, graces received and people met over the past week. Let us also remember all those in need of our prayers.

Introduction to the Scripture reading
Let us listen carefully to the Word of the Lord,
and attend to it with the ear of our hearts.
Let us welcome it, and faithfully put it into practice.

St. Benedict of Nursia (c.480-c.547) adapted

The Little Ones **Teach us, Lord**

Explore the Scriptures Luke 2:22-35

Note: While the story of Christ's birth is well known, his Presentation in the Temple is perhaps less familiar. For those living at the time, it would not have been unusual to see a young family bringing their first born to the Temple. In doing this, Mary and Joseph were affirming their Jewish faith, commemorating the Exodus event centuries before (Exodus 11-12).

That day, two humble individuals recognised our Saviour and revelled in the significance of his coming. Having devoted his life to worship, Scripture study and prayer, Simeon waited in patient expectation for the coming of the Lord, guided by the Psalms, the prayer book of Israel. Similarly, Anna had given her life to her faith, praying and fasting that God would fulfil his promises passed down the time of Abraham through the prophets. In doing so, their hearts and minds were undoubtedly open to the Lord. Having heard the Holy Spirit speaking to them, this aged man and woman recognised the importance of this young family, the Holy Family, when they approached the Temple that day.

When the time came for their purification according to the law of Moses, they brought him up to Jerusalem to present him to the Lord (as it is written in the law of the Lord, 'Every firstborn male shall be designated as holy to the Lord'), and they offered a sacrifice according to what is stated in the law of the Lord, 'a pair of turtle-doves or two young pigeons.'

Now there was a man in Jerusalem whose name was Simeon; this man was righteous and devout, looking forward to the consolation of Israel, and the Holy Spirit rested on him. It had been revealed to him by the Holy Spirit that he would not see death before he had seen the Lord's Messiah. Guided by the Spirit, Simeon came into the temple; and when the parents brought in the child Jesus, to do for him what was customary under the law, Simeon took him in his arms and praised God, saying, 'Master, now you are dismissing your servant in peace, according to your word; for my eyes have seen your salvation, which you have prepared in the presence of all peoples, a light for revelation to the Gentiles and for glory to your people Israel.'

And the child's father and mother were amazed at what was being said about him. Then Simeon blessed them and said to his mother Mary, 'This child is destined for the falling and the rising of many in Israel, and to be a sign that will be opposed so that the inner thoughts of many will be revealed—and a sword will pierce your own soul too.'

Please take a few moments in silence to reflect on the passage, then share a word or phrase that has struck you. Pause to think about what others have said then, after a second reading of the passage, you may wish to share a further thought.

Reflection

Like Mary and Joseph, new parents are, almost without exception, amazed by the birth of a child - awed by the miracle of life before them. How often do they gaze on those tiny hands and feet and wonder where those feet will tread or what those hands might make. Even earlier, from the moment of discovering that they have conceived a child, the man and the woman know that their lives will be changed forever - they are to be parents. Being blessed with this gift of a new life can also be a time of great uncertainty and perhaps even fear. As a young woman, although she trusted in the Lord, Mary must have felt something of this uncertainty on hearing that she would bear a son. However, without a moment's hesitation, she accepted God's call. 'In the faith of this humble handmaid, the Gift of God found the acceptance he had awaited from the beginning of time' (CCC, 2217).

Today, parents-to-be are encouraged to make all manner of preparations and given all sorts of advice from all sorts of people. As expectant parents, Mary and Joseph would not only have made such practical arrangements but would have made spiritual preparations: turning to the Lord in prayer. Praying for the child, before and after the birth, is important for contemporary parents too and the parish community have a share in this (see p.61 for a rite of blessing in the womb).

Shortly after Jesus' birth, his parents journeyed to the centuries-old centre for prayer, the Temple. There, Simeon foretold Christ's eventual suffering, death and resurrection and in doing so, he pointed directly to baptism, the sacrament of faith. From the time of the Early Church, parents wishing to pass on the gift of faith have presented their newly-born infants to the Church to be joined with Christ – not only dying with him but also reborn to a new and greater identity as a follower of Jesus Christ.

Blessing from day to day

The rite of infant baptism begins with the priest or deacon asking the parents what name they give their child. This sign of God's calling each of us by name to be joined with him for all eternity is then followed by a very powerful gesture. Claiming that child for Christ, the celebrant traces a cross on the child's forehead and both the parents and godparents are invited to do the same.

This gesture, symbolising the love of Jesus and the Trinitarian nature of our faith, can be done regularly by parents in the home to bless their child(ren) before bed and/or at the start of each day combined with the simple prayer: 'God bless you in the name of the Father, and the Son, and the Holy Spirit.' You could even make use of a sprinkling of holy water, available from your parish.

As the parents approach the font for the baptism of their child, what are they hoping and praying for? Health? Wealth? Happiness for their child? Fundamentally the prayer and the hope must be for 'happiness, not just in this world but for all eternity' (*Spe Salvi*, 7). From a tiny seed our capacity to believe, our faith, is nourished in this hope and aided by the gift of the Holy Spirit 'enabling [the baptised] to believe in God, to hope in him and to love him' (CCC, 1266).

As we reflect on the gift of new life, a new human being born into this world, we are reminded of God, our Father, author of all creation. However, even before the creation of the worlds (heaven and earth), the Father begot, that is brought forth his Son from himself, and gave everything he had to his natural son, Jesus (CCC, 246). In turn, loving without measure, through his suffering, death and resurrection, Jesus gave everything he had. He gave his life so that we would might have new life for all eternity as adopted sons and daughters of the divine Father. In response to this wondrous gift received at baptism we join with Christ in prayer to God, Our Father (CCC, 1243, 2789).

- *How often do we pray for other members of the Christian community?*
- *Although our baptism may have been decades ago, how do we recognise the importance of that day in our current stage of life?*
- *Do we recognise the importance of the gift of faith in our lives and give it the prominence it deserves?*

Closing Prayers
You may wish to end this session with the Lord's Prayer or silent reflection.

Lord, let me see your face,
know your heart
and experience your love in my life.
Strengthen in me the precious gift of faith.
I believe Lord;
Help my unbelief.
Amen.

Westminster Diocesan prayer for the Year of Faith (2012-2013)

Signpost

This session explored prayer for the unborn and newborn as the task of the whole community - a community strengthened by their presence. Next session we will look at the learning of prayer in childhood. Before the next session try to pray the Our Father, slowly, line by line, reflecting on its meaning. You may find page 58 useful.

2. Childhood

Then the whining schoolboy, with his satchel and shining morning face, creeping like snail unwillingly to school. William Shakespeare, As You Like It

This week we look at praying as children, mindful not to underestimate the depth of their innocent faith, and how we are able to move on in how we pray as we grow older. Children are capable of developing deep personal relationships with those who live far away as long as they hear about them frequently. So it is with us and God, invisible though ever-present.

Image: Jesus Among the Doctors by Éric de Saussure (1968)

Teach us, **Lord**

Childhood

Opening Prayers

Taken from Psalm 23(22) - to be said all together or the group can divide in half and alternate

All: In the name of the Father, and of the Son, and of the Holy Spirit. Amen.

A: The Lord is my shepherd, I shall not want.
He makes me lie down in green pastures;
he leads me beside still waters;
he restores my soul.
He leads me in right paths
for his name's sake.

B: Even though I walk through the darkest valley,
I fear no evil; for you are with me;
your rod and your staff -
they comfort me.

A: You prepare a table before me
in the presence of my enemies;
you anoint my head with oil;
my cup overflows.

B: Surely goodness and mercy shall follow me
all the days of my life,
and I shall dwell in the house of the Lord
my whole life long.

All: Glory be to the Father, and to the Son and to the Holy Spirit. As it was in
the beginning, is now, and ever shall be, world without end. Amen.

*As we come together let us, either aloud or in the silence of our hearts, give thanks
and praise to the Lord for all the things we have accomplished, the joys experienced,
graces received and people met over the past week. Let us also remember all those in
need of our prayers.*

Introduction to Reading of Scripture

Let us listen carefully to the Word of the Lord,
and attend to it with the ear of our hearts.
Let us welcome it, and faithfully put it into practice.

St. Benedict of Nursia (c.480-c.547) adapted

Explore the Scriptures Matthew 18:1-5, 10-14

Note: If we are truthful to ourselves, we don't want to be children - they can't vote or drive, they feel the pain of divorce and poverty without the ability to do anything about it. In this passage Jesus tells us to change, to become humble and surrender to God's will, and it is part of a wider discourse on the Church. What follows is more of Jesus' preaching on prayer and forgiveness.

At that time the disciples came to Jesus and asked, 'Who is the greatest in the kingdom of heaven?' He called a child, whom he put among them, and said, 'Truly I tell you, unless you change and become like children, you will never enter the kingdom of heaven. Whoever becomes humble like this child is the greatest in the kingdom of heaven. Whoever welcomes one such child in my name welcomes me.

'Take care that you do not despise one of these little ones; for, I tell you, in heaven their angels continually see the face of my Father in heaven. What do you think? If a shepherd has a hundred sheep, and one of them has gone astray, does he not leave the ninety-nine on the mountains and go in search of the one that went astray? And if he finds it, truly I tell you, he rejoices over it more than over the ninety-nine that never went astray. So it is not the will of your Father in heaven that one of these little ones should be lost.'

Please take a few moments in silence to reflect on the passage, then share a word or phrase that has struck you. Pause to think about what others have said then after a second reading of the passage you may wish to share a further thought.

Reflection

At a recent Mass I was stuck behind a pillar and was unable to see much of what was going on, however, I had a view that few other people had. On the side of the pillar, away from the majority of the people gathered, was one of the Stations of the Cross - Jesus falling for the first time.

I was struck at the time by how often children are unable to see the big event, too short to see over the heads of those in front (the same holds true for short adults too! See for instance Luke 19:1-10). That being said, children often have a view that the adults may not have or may miss. When Jesus fell for the first, the second and the third time those closer to the ground had a view of his face, those who had grown taller saw a fallen figure, the back of a head, a bloodied, disfigured convict.

Children so often have a different view of the world which matures and tends to conform to the way adults see it when they grow up. Jesus asks us to try our hardest to retain the child's perspective and to see the world like children – a view characterised by wonder and innocent love (Matthew 18:1-4).

Regarding prayer, children are able to understand the Lord in ways forgotten by the adults who care for them. It is important to teach children prayers – those we hold in common with the rest of the Christian community – but as, if not more, important is the ability to sustain and develop the natural loving relationship we each have with God from infancy. Like each of us, each child is different and will develop their faith in different ways. Some will explore prayer through music and art, others through the written word, yet more through touch and smell and gesture. It is good to have the simplicity of routine, repetition of prayers to help them become familiar, as well as time spent together but importantly we all need some form of 'spiritual space' to help in our personal growth and develop the personal relationship with Christ. We need to understand the words we use, making them our own, and explore the meaning of the gestures we make. Having the prayer life we desire requires that we yearn for God, whatever the words we say (CCC, 2558-9).

One key aspect to our faith, which we first encounter in childhood, is the realisation of the presence of Christ in the Eucharist. Many of the saints refer to moments in their childhood where they came to understand Jesus in the Eucharist and the impact this had on their lives (e.g. St Gemma Galgani and St. Thérèse of Lisieux). Most of us will remember the day of our First Communion but this relationship requires closer appreciation and further deepening; prayer before the Eucharist should form a major part of our 'spiritual space'.

Making room for God in your home or classroom

There are various bodily actions that we undertake when we enter a church: dipping our fingers into holy water as a reminder of our baptism, genuflecting at our pew to acknowledge the presence of the Lord in the tabernacle. Thoughts and actions combine.

Yet, our prayer life is not limited to those times in church. Environment has a large part to play in how we think and act, so setting aside a corner of a room at home or in the classroom can help us to lift our hearts and minds to the Lord, to respond to his love and to remind us of his presence in our lives. As simple as sacred images (such as an icon or religious painting), a candle, a crucifix placed on a shelf or small table can help us to disconnect from our work or play and to focus, for a few moments, on prayer.

Teach us, Lord Session Two

There is a maxim, often repeated in education circles, that you 'tell me and I forget, show me and I remember, involve me and I understand'. Just as we model faith for children, encouraging devotion, opening up the riches of faith, so we too can learn from the children we meet (see CCC, 2599). We must be conscious that faith, enlivened and sustained by prayer is not a condition to be taken for granted, but rather a gift of God [which] needs to be nourished and reinforced' so that it can continue to guide us on our pilgrim way (*Lumen Fidei*, 6).

- *What might be the difference between being taught prayers and learning how to pray?*
- *Who taught you how to pray?*
- *How might we personally foster the 'childlike' view of the world of which Christ talks? How do we maintain an attitude of wonder and awe at God's creation and love?*
- *How can our homes reflect our Christian faith?*

Closing Prayers
You may wish to end this session with some different prayers or silent reflection.

Lord, let me see your face,
know your heart
and experience your love in my life.
Strengthen in me the precious gift of faith.
I believe Lord;
Help my unbelief.
Amen.

Westminster Diocesan prayer for the Year of Faith (2012-2013)

Signpost

This session looked at how we might learn how to pray and that this learning can take a lifetime. Next session will look prayer as a conversation in love with God. Before the next session you might wish to take one of your favourite prayers and say it very slowly, line by line, reflecting on each phrase. Also try to read *Catechism* paragraph 2599.

3. Youth

And then the lover, sighing like furnace, with a woeful ballad made to his mistress' eyebrow.
William Shakespeare, As You Like It

This week we look at prayer as a conversation in love with the Father. The Scriptures can be read as a love story between the Creator and his creation; in this session we will read from the Song of Songs which demonstrates this beautifully. We will also look at how gestures help us in our understanding and practice of prayer.

Image: The Marriage Feast at Cana by Hieronymous Bosch (post-1550)

Youth

Opening prayer
Taken from the Song of Songs, chapter 2. Very often in surveys of those in religious life, the Song of Songs comes top in terms of Scripture passages that are considered fruitful for meditation and prayer.

All: In the name of the Father, and of the Son, and of the Holy Spirit. Amen.

A: I am the rose of Sharon, the lily of the valleys.
As a lily among the thistles, so is my beloved among girls.
As an apple tree among the trees of the wood,
so is my love among young men.

B: In his delightful shade I sit, and his fruit is sweet to my taste.
He has taken me to his cellar, and his banner over me is love.
Feed me with raisin cakes, restore me with apples, for I am sick with love.
His left arm is under my head, his right embraces me.

A: I charge you, daughters of Jerusalem,
by all gazelles and wild does, do not rouse,
do not wake my beloved before she pleases.

B: I hear my love.
See how he comes leaping on the mountains, bounding over the hills.
My love is like a gazelle, like a young stag.
See where he stands behind our wall.
He looks in at the window, he peers through the opening.

A: My love lifts up his voice,
he says to me, 'Come then, my beloved, my lovely one, come.
For see, winter is past, the rains are over and gone.
'Flowers are appearing on the earth.

B: The season of glad songs has come,
the cooing of the turtledove is heard in our land.
My love is mine and I am his.

All: Glory be to the Father, and to the Son and to the Holy Spirit. As it was in the beginning, is now, and ever shall be, world without end. Amen.

As we come together let us, either aloud or in the silence of our hearts, give thanks and praise to the Lord for all the things we have accomplished, the joys experienced, graces received and people met over the past week. Let us also remember all those in need of our prayers.

Introduction to Reading of Scripture
Let us listen carefully to the Word of the Lord,
and attend to it with the ear of our hearts.
Let us welcome it, and faithfully put it into practice.

St. Benedict of Nursia (c.480-c.547) adapted

Explore the Scriptures Luke 10:38-42

Note: Immediately prior to this episode, before setting off for Caesarea Philippi, Jesus had cured a blind man at Bethsaida. Six days later, Peter, James and John were to experience the wonder of Jesus' transfiguration on Mount Tabor (an event remembered with joy by Peter in his second letter addressed to 'all who treasure the same faith as ourselves, given through the righteousness of our God and saviour Jesus Christ' – 2 Peter 1:16-18).

Now as they went on their way, he entered a certain village, where a woman named Martha welcomed him into her home. She had a sister named Mary, who sat at the Lord's feet and listened to what he was saying. But Martha was distracted by her many tasks; so she came to him and asked, 'Lord, do you not care that my sister has left me to do all the work by myself? Tell her then to help me.' But the Lord answered her, 'Martha, Martha, you are worried and distracted by many things; there is need of only one thing. Mary has chosen the better part, which will not be taken away from her.'

Please take a few moments in silence to reflect on the passage, then share a word or phrase that has struck you. Pause to think about what others have said then after a second reading of the passage you may wish to share a further thought.

Reflection
The joy and love that a man and a woman express publicly on their wedding day is shared by everyone in attendance. Falling in love is an experience that might be recent for some of us and something that happened a long time ago for others. It is wonderful to feel that connection with another person whether it is instantaneous or something to which you came to a gradual realisation. With it come feelings of excitement, completeness and passion. Your every moment seems taken up with the thought of that person. They become the centre of your existence and worldview and it is a moment of pure gift, one to the other.

God desires this kind of relationship with each of us. A rarely quoted book of the Old Testament – the Song of Songs – illustrates this beautifully. The poems in this book were originally love-songs and express passionately, not just the love between two lovers, but the true love that exists between God and his people (*Deus Caritas Est*, 6). This divinely intended relationship finds its fulfillment in total self-gift, one to the other, as each seeks the good of their 'beloved', even if it means renunciation and sacrifice.

Human beings are made for this loving relationship and that is essentially what prayer is – being in a loving relationship with the God who made us. This relationship was expressed when God created the first man and woman (Genesis 1), then later he chose a people – the people of Israel – to love passionately and that his love might be returned. He made a covenant with the Jews as a Bridegroom to a Bride (Hosea 2:16-24) and so too, today, the Church is often described as God's 'Bride' (CCC, 823). Throughout Salvation History – from Adam and Eve, through to the covenant made with the Jews and then the Church – we can begin to understand how the love story between God and his people has unfolded, and continues to unfold.

We, ourselves, enter this relationship through the sacraments and are sustained in it through prayer. In John's account of the passage from Luke which we shared earlier, he records Mary's seemingly indulgent action of anointing Jesus' feet with expensive ointment (John 12:1-3). In a very real way this was a form of prayer. She wanted to spend time with Jesus and lovingly responded to the source of pure love that was before her, by showing her love for Him through a simple and pure gesture of adoration.

Displaying our love of God in both word and symbol is central to Catholic prayer and it can be helpful sometimes to put our prayer book to one side to explore

What is recollection?
What the three major expressions of the life of prayer (vocal prayer, meditation, and contemplative prayer) have in common is the recollection of the heart (CCC, 2721).

To recollect is to mentally set aside the busy-ness of our daily lives and to open our hearts and minds to the presence of our loving God. Being unseen, the wondrous gift of the Holy Spirit, given to each of us at baptism, can seem distant or even forgotten. Each time we begin to pray, it is important to remind ourselves of his ever presence in the depths of our souls.

Some may find those first waking moments of the day – before our senses and minds are bombarded with sights, sounds and thoughts – as the ideal time to spend a bit of time with the Lord. Others may prefer to take time as the night falls.

different ways of conversing with God. St Dominic, for example, was a man who was deeply in love with God and he taught nine ways of prayer including standing, bowing and kneeling. He understood that gestures of the body could help people to pray and to lift up all that they are and have to the Lord (see p.56).

The reality of the ongoing love story between God and his people was dramatically witnessed when 80,000 people knelt in adoration of the Blessed Sacrament at Hyde Park during Benedict XVI's visit in 2010. Stillness filled that space. It was a moment of God, Our Beloved, gazing on his people. We in turn returned that loving gaze, echoing the prayer in the Song of Songs, 'My love is mine and I am his'.

- *Naturally, relationships have their ups and downs - and with prayer we can experience periods of dryness and periods of joy - but the importance of earnest, honest and constant communication cannot be understated. How honest am I in my prayer?*
- *How and when have I felt the love of God?*
- *How often am I able to make time for prayer?*
- *What gestures do I find helpful in my prayer?*

Closing Prayers
You may wish to end this session this poem or with different prayers or silent reflection.

Nothing is more practical than finding God,
than falling in Love in a quite absolute, final way.
What you are in love with,
what seizes your imagination, will affect everything.
It will decide what will get you out of bed in the morning,
what you do with your evenings,
how you spend your weekends,
what you read, whom you know,
what breaks your heart,
and what amazes you with joy and gratitude.
Fall in Love, stay in love, and it will decide everything.

attributed to Fr Pedro Arrupe SJ (1907-1991)

Signpost

This session looked at the ongoing love story between God and humanity. Prayer is, in essence, an offering to and receiving from God in love. Next session will explore prayer in relation to the tasks we perform on a daily basis. Before then, read the Archbishop's foreword (p.3) and think who you know who might benefit from taking part in your group.

4. Maturing In Our Faith

Then a soldier, full of strange oaths and bearded like the pard, jealous in honour, sudden and quick in quarrel, seeking the bubble reputation even in the cannon's mouth. William Shakespeare, As You Like It

This week we look at the stage in life where we know more about who we are and look to make our mark on the world. The session also explores the relationship between prayer, work and charitable action, acknowledging the need to seek God's will in all things.

Image: The Good Samaritan wood carving from Our Lady Queen of the Most Holy Rosary Cathedral, Toledo, Ohio

Teach us, **Lord**

Maturing in Our Faith

Opening prayer

Taken from Psalm 138(137) - to be said all together or the group can divide in half and alternate

All: In the name of the Father, and of the Son, and of the Holy Spirit. Amen.

A: Praise the Lord!
Happy are those who fear the Lord,
who greatly delight in his commandments.

B: I give you thanks, O Lord, with my whole heart;
I bow down towards your holy temple
and give thanks to your name for your steadfast love and your faithfulness;

A: On the day I called, you answered me,
you increased my strength of soul.

B: All the kings of the earth shall praise you, O Lord,
for they have heard the words of your mouth.
For though the Lord is high, he regards the lowly;
but the haughty he perceives from far away.

A: Though I walk in the midst of trouble,
you preserve me against the wrath of my enemies;
you stretch out your hand,
and your right hand delivers me.

B: The Lord will fulfil his purpose for me;
your steadfast love, O Lord, endures for ever.
Do not forsake the work of your hands.

All: Glory be to the Father, and to the Son and to the Holy Spirit. As it was in
the beginning, is now, and ever shall be, world without end. Amen.

*As we come together let us, either aloud or in the silence of our hearts, give thanks
and praise to the Lord for all the things we have accomplished, the joys experienced,
graces received and people met over the past week. Let us also remember all those in
need of our prayers.*

Introduction to Reading of Scripture

Let us pray with great confidence, with confidence based upon the goodness and infinite generosity of God and upon the promises of Jesus Christ. God is a spring of living water which flows unceasingly into the hearts of those who pray.

St Louis de Montfort (1673-1716)

Explore the Scriptures Matthew 5:1-12, 15-16

Note: The Beatitudes (Latin for 'happy' but here translated as 'blessed') are teachings of Jesus found in the Gospels of Matthew and Luke. They show a condition or way of life and what results and they echo Jesus' other teachings on mercy, compassion and fortitude. They also reflect passages from the Old Testament such as Isaiah 51:7. After the Sermon on the Mount, of which this passage forms a part, Matthew goes on to recount ten miracles performed by Jesus.

When Jesus saw the crowds, he went up the mountain; and after he sat down, his disciples came to him. Then he began to speak, and taught them, saying:

'Blessed are the poor in spirit, for theirs is the kingdom of heaven.

Blessed are those who mourn, for they will be comforted.

Blessed are the meek, for they will inherit the earth.

Blessed are those who hunger and thirst for righteousness, for they will be filled.

Blessed are the merciful, for they will receive mercy.

Blessed are the pure in heart, for they will see God.

Blessed are the peacemakers, for they will be called children of God.

Blessed are those who are persecuted for righteousness' sake, for theirs is the kingdom of heaven.

Blessed are you when people revile you and persecute you and utter all kinds of evil against you falsely on my account. Rejoice and be glad, for your reward is great in heaven, for in the same way they persecuted the prophets who were before you.

You are the light of the world. A city built on a hill cannot be hidden. No one after lighting a lamp puts it under the bushel basket, but on the lampstand, and it gives light to all in the house. In the same way, let your light shine before others, so that they may see your good works and give glory to your Father in heaven.'

Please take a few moments in silence to reflect on the passage, then share a word or phrase that has struck you. Pause to think about what others have said then after a second reading of the passage you may wish to share a further thought.

Reflection

For many of us there is a deep desire to be remembered for something positive. As such, making our mark in the world is closely linked to the work we do with and for others, whether in the family or the wider community including that of the Church. Though St Matthew may write 'give your gifts in secret' it is always nice to be noticed for the good that we do and the love that we are able to show (Matthew 6:4-6). Whether the accomplishments we achieve or the help we give others comes from paid employment, from charitable activity or from simple acts of kindness from day to day, our lives and our work are fed by prayer and, in turn, 'prayer translates our work into closer union with God and a deeper understanding of the world around us' (*Youcat*, 494).

Each Lent we are reminded of the relationship between prayer, fasting and almsgiving. We fast to deny ourselves such pleasures which can distract us from prayer and a simpler life leads us deeper into a loving relationship with God. So too, the money and the time we save in such simplicity can be used to support those in need. In all this, our charitable activity and our life at work and home should be guided by the faith which works through love (*Deus Caritas Est*, 28 & 33).

Matthew Kelly in his book *Rediscover Catholicism* writes about the ability to transform everyday activities into prayer, one hour at a time, one task at a time:

'A man's work may be to collect trash, but if he does it well, and hour by hour turns to God in his heart and says, Father I offer you this hour of work as a prayer for my neighbour Karen who is struggling with cancer… or in thanksgiving for my wife and children, then he has truly discovered and is living the words "pray constantly" (1 Thessalonians 5:17).'

Types of Prayer: Vocal

Vocal prayer, founded on the union of body and soul in human nature, associates the body with the interior prayer of the heart, following Christ's example of praying to his Father and teaching the Our Father to his disciples (CCC, 2722).

Our prayer life can become routine, consisting of a quick recitation of the prayers we learned in childhood. Whether prayers are said with others in church, with family in our homes or even quietly spoken while walking down the street, it is important to guard against emptiness – the tendency to mouth the words, with their meanings largely forgotten and our minds concentrating on other matters.

To help, perhaps we can visualise Christ on the Cross. We might also explore the reflections on the Our Father in *Youcat* (514-527) and the *Catechism of the Catholic Church* (CCC 2777- 2855).

This is not new! Centuries ago St John Chrysostom talked of this when he said:

> 'Our soul should be directed in God, not merely when we suddenly think of prayer, but even when we are concerned with something else. If we are looking after the poor, if we are busy in some other way, or if we are doing any type of good work, we should season our actions with the desire and the remembrance of God. Through this salt of the love of God we can all become a sweet dish for the Lord. If we are generous in giving time to prayer, we will experience its benefits throughout our life.'

Such a transformation of the ordinary tasks we do into prayer is the very essence of the interior life and a chance to encounter God. Whether we are washing the dishes or studying for an exam, by offering these actions to God as a prayer they become noble tasks, a form of spiritual exercise that draws us nearer to God (see Ephesians 2:10). As we grow in age, through work, we come to understand that prayer is not simply time apart from activity – though that is vital – if done in the right frame of mind and with the right intention, activity can be prayer itself.

- *For what do you wish to be remembered?*
- *How often do you refer to the life and teachings of Jesus before performing a task or making a decision?*
- *How are you able to extend prayer into the everyday?*

Closing Prayers

You may wish to end this session with different prayers, for example the reflection based on the Beatitudes on p.59 or silent reflection.

Lord, teach me to seek you, and reveal yourself to me when I seek you.
For I cannot seek you unless you first teach me,
nor find you, unless you first reveal yourself to me.
Let me seek you in longing, and long for you in seeking.
Let me find you in love, and love you in finding.
Amen.

St Ambrose of Milan (c.340-397)

Signpost

This session looked at how we might pray echoing Colossians 3:17 - 'Whatsoever you do in word or in work, do all in the name of the Lord Jesus Christ.' Next session we will look at middle age and the opportunity to assess our life's work. Between now and the next session try to make a daily offering as part of your routine (see p.62).

5. Full of Wisdom

And then the justice, in fair round belly with good capon lined, with eyes severe and beard of formal cut, full of wise saws and modern instances; and so he plays his part. William Shakespeare, As You Like It

This week we look at middle age, a time when many are thinking of retirement and a life of relative ease. This can be approached as an opportunity to reassess where we are, to take up new challeneges and approach our pursuit of sainthood with renewed vigour.

Image: The Pharisee and Tax Collector wood carving from Our Lady Queen of the Most Holy Rosary Cathedral, Toledo, Ohio

Full of Wisdom

Opening prayer
Taken from the Book of Wisdom 6:12-20

All: In the name of the Father, and of the Son, and of the Holy Spirit. Amen.

A: Wisdom is radiant and unfading,
and she is easily discerned by those who love her,
and is found by those who seek her.

B: She hastens to make herself known to those who desire her.
One who rises early to seek her will have no difficulty,
for she will be found sitting at the gate.

A: To fix one's thought on her is perfect understanding,
and one who is vigilant on her account will soon be free from care,
because she goes about seeking those worthy of her,
and she graciously appears to them in their paths,
and meets them in every thought.

B: The beginning of wisdom is the most sincere desire for instruction,
and concern for instruction is love of her,

A: and love of her is the keeping of her laws,
and giving heed to her laws is assurance of immortality,
and immortality brings one near to God;
so the desire for wisdom leads to a kingdom.

All: Glory be to the Father, and to the Son and to the Holy Spirit. As it was in
the beginning, is now, and ever shall be, world without end. Amen.

*As we come together let us, either aloud or in the silence of our hearts, give thanks
and praise to the Lord for all the things we have accomplished, the joys experienced,
graces received and people met over the past week. Let us also remember all those in
need of our prayers.*

Introduction to Reading of Scripture
Let us go forward in peace, our eyes upon heaven, the only one goal of our labours.
St Thérèse of Lisieux (1873-1897)

Explore the Scriptures Luke 18:9-14

Note: St Luke's Gospel contains a number of parables told by Christ. In these parables, Christ referred to people and events commonly known at the time to exemplify a message - a teaching that he wished to pass on to his followers. A sect of Jewish people known as the Pharisees, who lived in the time of Christ, strived to live orderly lives according to the precepts known as The Law. On the other hand, tax collectors where not at all well regarded at that time. They were generally viewed as greedy individuals who made their living by imposing surcharges on the taxes they collected on behalf of the Roman Empire. St Matthew was a tax collector (publican) when Jesus called him to become an Apostle.

He also told this parable to some who trusted in themselves that they were righteous and regarded others with contempt: 'Two men went up to the temple to pray, one a Pharisee and the other a tax collector. The Pharisee, standing by himself, was praying thus, "God, I thank you that I am not like other people: thieves, rogues, adulterers, or even like this tax collector. I fast twice a week; I give a tenth of all my income." But the tax collector, standing far off, would not even look up to heaven, but was beating his breast and saying, "God, be merciful to me, a sinner!" I tell you, this man went down to his home justified rather than the other; for all who exalt themselves will be humbled, but all who humble themselves will be exalted.'

Please take a few moments in silence to reflect on the passage, then share a word or phrase that has struck you. Pause to think about what others have said then after a second reading of the passage you may wish to share a further thought.

Reflection

After years of hard work, the prospects of retirement may seem quite enticing! Travel, volunteer commitments, family gatherings, new exercise regimes, a bit of gardening and social engagements would fill the days. It would be a time to look back and take pride in past accomplishments and the material comforts that have been hard earned over time. However, is this really a time to quietly slip into complacency, feeling relatively secure; comfortably enjoying the fruits of our labours or is it a time to think afresh? Is this, in reality, an opportunity to contemplate the hand of God in and through our lives?

Following their liberation from slavery in Egypt, during a long and arduous journey, the Israelites grew impatient with Moses and with God and sought comfort in the work of their own hands, a golden calf (Exodus 32). In his recent encyclical, *Lumen Fidei*, Pope Francis writes about this inability to 'endure the time of waiting to see the face of God' and the pride they showed in 'setting themselves at the centre of reality and worshipping the work of their own hands' (LF, 13).

Teach us, Lord Session Five

The messengers of the Lord, the prophets, had to continually remind the Israelites of turn back to God to seek his mercy and forgiveness, his help and protection in times of draught, famine and war. Those times when they raised their hearts and minds back to God, they were fed or saved from the wrath of their enemies. Although they experienced first hand the fruits of their prayers, they too sometimes struggled to make them a part of their life in the good times - to remember God with prayers of praise and thanksgiving.

From another era, St Luke's Gospel recounts Christ's teaching about the Pharisee and the publican (a collector of tax) visiting the synagogue, the Jewish House of prayer. Like his ancestors, the Pharisee takes matters into his own hands and puts his case before God with a lengthy list of accomplishments substantiating his own self-worth. Setting forth all his good works in compliance with The Law, this self-made man judged himself a much better Jew than others around him. In sharp contrast, the publican stood back keenly aware of his faults and failings; awed by the depths of God's mercy and forgiveness.

The Pharisee would have known the prayers of his forefathers, the Psalms, that had been handed down from David, Isaiah among others. Their words would have undoubtedly passed his lips but were they the type of prayer which St John Damascene described as 'the raising of one's mind and heart to God' (CCC, 2590)? The publican, on the other hand, humbled himself and spoke from the heart.

Such humility may seem out of step in the current age where self-assuredness and independence are highly valued. Yet, in his parable, Christ points to the humble man, the tax collector, as a model for prayer.

Types of Prayer: Meditation

Meditation is a prayerful quest engaging thought, imagination, emotion, and desire. Its goal is to make our own in faith the subject considered, by confronting it with our own life (CCC, 2723).

In October 2012, Pope Emeritus Benedict XVI declared St John of Ávila a Doctor of the Church (one whose writings and sermons are relevant to Christians of any era). This master spiritual director from the 16th century suggests that persons who 'desire to grow in intimacy with the Lord learn to meditate – to join in a loving conversation with our Creator.' While meditation may take various forms, in his classic work, *Audi, filia*, St John proposes that we begin by reading a passage of Holy Scripture or gazing upon a sacred image. The objective is to focus the mind on the story of our salvation and the life of Christ- and to **think** about them.

Full of Wisdom **Teach us, Lord**

While in her sixties and already having published numerous books and led reforms to monasteries in the Spanish church, St Teresa of Ávila was asked to write yet another book on prayer. In her spiritual classic, *The Interior Castle*, this great mystic, who became a Doctor of the Church in 1970, reminds us that humility is foundational for prayer. Prayer begins with 'knowing the greatness of God' and 'cultivating a discipline of humility and self-knowledge'. While we may have amassed vast amounts of worldly knowledge, it is important to 'set our eyes on Christ' to get to know to whom we are praying and to reflect on our own selves in light of his glory: 'by glimpsing his greatness, we recognise our own powerlessness; gazing upon his purity, we notice where we are impure, pondering his humility, we see how far from humble we are.'

Questions
- *Where have you experienced the greatness of God?*
- *Have you undergone a period of dryness in prayer? What helped you to get through it?*
- *How has the way we pray changed over the course of our life?*
- *How may we be able to develop a 'discipline of humilty and self-knowledge'?*
- *What might I try differently in my prayer as a result of these weeks of sharing?*

Closing Prayers
You may wish to end this session with some different prayers or silent reflection.

Let nothing upset you,
let nothing startle you.
All things pass;
God does not change.
Patience wins
all it seeks.
Whoever has God
lacks nothing:
God alone is enough.
Amen.

St Teresa of Ávila (1515-1582)

Signpost This session looked at the challenges posed by material comfort and a degree of respectability. In practical terms our prayer should be characterised by humility. Each day is a new chance to head out on the road to sainthood. Next session will look at old age and prayer. Before then have a look at pages 51 to 55 and pick out your 3 favourite quotes.

6. Close to the Father

The sixth age shifts into the lean and slippered pantaloon, with spectacles on nose and pouch on side; his youthful hose, well saved, a world too wide for his shrunk shank, and his big manly voice, turning again toward childish treble, pipes and whistles in his sound. Last scene of all, that ends this strange eventful history, is second childishness and mere oblivion, sans teeth, sans eyes, sans taste, sans everything. William Shakespeare, As You Like It

This week we look at old age, a time when, despite our frailty and dependency, we can profoundly witness to God's loving presence and to the expectant hope of eternal life. Such hope and the desire to do God's will can come to each of us, throughout life, as a fruit of prayer.

Image: King David Playing the Harp by Gerrit van Honthorst (1611)

Teach us, **Lord**

Close to the Father

Opening prayer

Taken from Psalm 72(71) - to be said all together or the group can divide in half and alternate

All: In the name of the Father, and of the Son, and of the Holy Spirit. Amen.

A: You, O Lord, are my hope, my trust, O Lord, from my youth.
Upon you I have leaned from my birth;
it was you who took me from my mother's womb.
My praise is continually of you.

B: My mouth is filled with your praise,
and with your glory all day long.
Do not cast me off in the time of old age;
do not forsake me when my strength is spent.

A: But I will hope continually,
and will praise you yet more and more.
My mouth will tell of your righteous acts,
of your deeds of salvation all day long,

B: O God, from my youth you have taught me,
and I still proclaim your wondrous deeds.
So even to old age and grey hairs,
O God, do not forsake me,

A: You who have done great things,
O God, who is like you?
You who have made me see many troubles will revive me again.
You will increase my honour, and comfort me once again.

All: Glory be to the Father, and to the Son and to the Holy Spirit. As it was in
the beginning, is now, and ever shall be, world without end. Amen.

*As we come together let us, either aloud or in the silence of our hearts, give thanks
and praise to the Lord for all the things we have accomplished, the joys experienced,
graces received and people met over the past week. Let us also remember all those in
need of our prayers.*

Introduction to Reading of Scripture

Christ be with me, Christ within me, Christ behind me, Christ before me, Christ beside me, Christ to win me, Christ to comfort me and restore me.

attributed to St. Patrick (c.387 – 493 or c.460)

Explore the Scriptures John 21:16-19

Note: This is the last chapter of St John's Gospel, in the form of an appendix, and chronicles the appearance of Jesus on Lake Tiberias. The three proclamations of love by Peter bring to mind his threefold denial of Christ immediately prior to the Crucifixion.

Jesus said to Simon Peter, 'Simon son of John, do you love me more than these others do?' He answered, 'Yes, Lord, you know I love you.' Jesus said to him, 'Feed my lambs.'

A second time he said to him, 'Simon son of John, do you love me?' He replied, 'Yes, Lord, you know I love you.' Jesus said to him, 'Look after my sheep.'

Then he said to him a third time, 'Simon son of John, do you love me?' Peter was hurt that he asked him a third time, 'Do you love me?' and said, 'Lord, you know everything; you know I love you.' Jesus said to him, 'Feed my sheep.

In all truth I tell you, when you were young you put on your own belt and walked where you liked; but when you grow old you will stretch out your hands, and somebody else will put a belt round you and take you where you would rather not go.' In these words he indicated the kind of death by which Peter would give glory to God. After this he said, 'Follow me.'

Please take a few moments in silence to reflect on the passage, then share a word or phrase that has struck you. Pause to think about what others have said then after a second reading of the passage you may wish to share a further thought.

Reflection

Just as the Lord loves us from the moment of our conception, so his gracious care follows us throughout our life and beyond (see opening prayer). As we near the end of our life here on earth, uncertainty can fill our days – good health may weaken, skills may diminish and status within the family and community can change. Some become totally dependent on others, invisible in social situations, overlooked and unheard. Sometimes too they are taken where they would rather not go (John 21:18). In all of this, however, our value never changes in the sight of God and 'recognising dependence with respect to the Creator is a source of wisdom and freedom, of joy and confidence' (CCC, 301).

When Jesus asks Peter if he loves him, the three questions posed are extremely searching. Jesus is delving with each question into the depths of Peter's heart. He is exploring what and who it is that Peter loves the most. In his responses Peter is submitting his will and professing his total love of and commitment to Christ. Although Peter didn't know it then, love meant laying down his life for his faith (1 John 3:16). So too, in the final days of our life, our answer to the questions that Jesus asked of Peter will have eternal consequences. Old age is a time of decision to choose Goodness and Love to the end.

In Blessed John Paul II's 1999 Letter to the Elderly he reminds us that old age can become life-giving if 'we reach out and grasp the hands of Christ' (7). Old age is an opportunity to recall, with gratitude, a life gifted by God. It can be a time for patient recollection, thanksgiving and a deepening of prayer. Where we may not be able to serve those around us in practical ways, we can share God's love through gesture and word, 'instilling courage by loving advice, silent prayers, or even witness of suffering borne with patient acceptance' (13).

Old age is a time when we are further along in the pilgrimage to God than most of those younger than us. It is a time when, despite our frailty and dependency, we can profoundly witness to God's loving presence and to the expectant hope of eternal life. We learn, throughout the course of our lives, all kinds of things and facts but we also learn to hope and prayer is truly the 'school of hope' (*Spe Salvi*, 32). St Augustine wrote of the need for our heart to stretch, that through our life-long desire for God we may increase our heart's capacity for receiving God's goodness. Prayer is, therefore, a place where we learn to place our hope in God and it is an exercise where we train our heart in both giving and receiving love.

Types of Prayer: Contemplation

Contemplative prayer is the simple expression of the mystery of prayer. It is a gaze of faith fixed on Jesus, an attentiveness to the Word of God, a silent love. It achieves real union with the prayer of Christ to the extent that it makes us share in his mystery (CCC 2724).

Just as friendships deepen over time and it becomes possible to enjoy the company of a loved one without the need for continual conversation, prayers of meditation (essentially our effort) can evolve into those of contemplation. St Teresa of Ávila, doctor of the Church, wrote extensively about this more passive and receptive form of prayer. In her classic work, *The Interior Castle,* St Teresa applies the image of a castle to a life of prayer that culminates in the innermost dwelling, in intimacy with our Lord and King. Mindful of the importance of calm and quiet, she explains the life of prayer as a journey that requires faith, humility and perseverance to overcome our worldly desires and to conform ourselves in all things to the will of God.

I remember visiting an elderly relative for years and was deeply moved by the fact that her Catholic prayer book was never far from her side. The habit of prayer and her personal relationship with Christ sustained her. Despite her loneliness, she exuded joy that came from knowing, like Peter, she was loved by God. Even though her physical prowess had waned, each time I visited her she fed me with Christian wisdom through the sharing some simple advice or a kind word. We don't have to wait until we're old to start asking for the spiritual maturity and wisdom associated with old age. We can stretch our hearts now – asking the Father, Son and Holy Spirit for this, today, through prayer.

Questions

- *How has the prayerful witness of an older person inspired you on your faith journey?*
- *Where have you witnessed to our faith to someone younger whether in your family or in the wider parish community?*
- *How might we better value the contribution and wisdom of the elderly in society and in the Church?*
- *What do you think it means to be 'dependent on God'?*

Closing Prayers

You may wish to end this session with some different prayers or silent reflection.

Eternal Father,
your Son has promised that whatever we ask in his name will be given to us.
In his name I pray:
give me a burning faith, a joyful hope, a holy love for Jesus Christ.

Give me the grace of perseverance in doing your will in all things.
Do with me what you will.
I repent of having offended you.
Grant, O Lord, that I may love you always and never let me be separated from you.

O my God and my All, make me a saint!
Amen.

St Alphonsus Maria de Liguori (1696–1787)

Signpost

This session explored prayer in old age and the wisdom which can nourish society and the Church found therein. Remember in between faith-sharing seasons, additional sessions and reflections can be found on dowsmallgroups.wordpress.com. Going on, try to find time to read Pope Francis' Angelus address July 2013 from Rio http://goo.gl/qLlGdd

Daily Prayer: **Sunday to Saturday**

'The Office is... the prayer of the whole People of God.' Apostolic Constitution, Canticum Laudis

The daily prayers on the following pages are drawn from the Divine Office (Liturgy of the Hours). Together with the Mass, the Office constitutes the official public prayer life of the Church. It is celebrated in both the Eastern and Western Churches. The Office is intended to be read communally but here we invite you to use it as a personal daily prayer. Each day contains a hymn, a Scripture reading, a psalm or canticle and a selection of prayers.

Image: Apparition of the Virgin to St Bernard by Filippino Lippi (1480)

Teach us, Lord

Sunday - Sing a New Song

Introduction
O God, come to our aid. Lord, make haste to help us.

Glory be to the Father and to the Son and to the Holy Spirit, as it was in the beginning, is now, and ever shall be, world without end. Amen. (Alleluia)
omit Alleluias during Lent

Hymn
O blessèd Lord, Creator God,
In you all things are rendered pure,
By you are strengthened to endure.

O blessèd, holy hand of God,
All things are sanctified by you;
Adorned, enriched, you make them new.

O blessèd, Majesty of God,
Containing all that you have filled;
All things are done as you have willed.

O blessèd, holy Trinity,
Serene and certain in your ways;
You are the light of endless days.

Antiphon
I will bless you all my life, Lord; in your name I will lift up my hands.

Psalmody   *Psalm 149*
Sing a new song to the Lord,
his praise in the assembly of the faithful.
Let Israel rejoice in its Maker,
let Zion's sons exult in their king.
Let them praise his name with dancing
and make music with timbrel and harp.

For the Lord takes delight in his people.
He crowns the poor with salvation.
Let the faithful rejoice in their glory,
shout for joy and take their rest.
Let the praise of God be on their lips
and a two-edged sword in their hand,

to deal out vengeance to the nations
and punishment on all the peoples;
to bind their kings in chains
and their nobles in fetters of iron;
to carry out the sentence pre-ordained:
this honour is for all his faithful.

Glory be…

Antiphon
I will bless you all my life, Lord; in your name I will lift up my hands.

Reading   *Revelation 7:10-12*
Victory to our God, who sits on the throne, and to the Lamb! Praise and glory and wisdom and thanksgiving and honour and power and strength to our God for ever and ever. Amen.

Short Responsory
℟ Rejoice in the Lord, O you just; for praise is fitting for loyal hearts.
℣ Sing to him a new song. ℟
Glory be… ℟

Benedictus/Magnificat Antiphon
Whoever does the will of God is my brother, and my sister, and my mother.

Benedictus (if said in the morning) or Magnificat (if said in the evening) - see inside back cover for these prayers

Intercessions
Let us pray to Christ the Lord, the sun who enlightens us all, whose light will never fail us.
℟ Lord our Saviour, give us life!

Lord of the sun and the stars, lead us by your Spirit to do your will; guide and pretect us by your wisdom.
℟ Lord our Saviour, give us life!

Lord, grant us your gifts, though we are unworthy; with all our hearts we thank you.
℟ Lord our Saviour, give us life!

Lord, help us to bring your compassion to the poor, the sick, the lonely, the unloved; lead us to find you in every day.
℟ Lord our Saviour, give us life!

Our Father…

Concluding prayer
Lord God,
since by the adoption of grace,
you have made us children of light:
do not let false doctrine darken
  our minds,
but grant that your light may shine
  within us
and we may always live in the brightness
  of truth.
Through Christ our Lord.
Amen.

Assumption of the Virgin by
Francesco Granacci (c.1520)

Monday – The Splendour of his Name

Introduction
O God, come to our aid. Lord, make haste to help us.

Glory be to the Father and to the Son and to the Holy Spirit, as it was in the beginning, is now, and ever shall be, world without end. Amen. (Alleluia)
omit Alleluias during Lent

Hymn
The day is filled with splendour
When God brings light from light,
And all renewed creation
Rejoices in his sight.

The Father gives his children
The wonder of the world
In which his power and glory
Like banners are unfurled.

With every living creature,
Awaking with the day,
We turn to God our Father,
Lift up our hearts and pray:

O Father, Son and Spirit,
Your grace and mercy send,
That we may live to praise you
Today and to the end.

Antiphon
Lord our God, we praise the splendour of your name.

Psalmody *Psalm 29(28)*
O give the Lord, you sons of God,
give the Lord glory and power;
give the Lord the glory of his name.
Adore the Lord in his holy court.

The Lord's voice resounding on the waters,
the Lord on the immensity of waters;
the voice of the Lord, full of power,
the voice of the Lord, full of splendour.

The Lord's voice shattering the cedars,
the Lord shatters the cedars of Lebanon;
he makes Lebanon leap like a calf
and Sirion like a young wild ox.

The Lord's voice shaking the wilderness,
the Lord shakes the wilderness of Kadesh;
the Lord's voice rending the oak tree
and stripping the forest bare.

The God of glory thunders.
In his temple they all cry: 'Glory!'
The Lord sat enthroned over the flood;
the Lord sits as king for ever.

The Lord will give strength to his people,
the Lord will bless his people with peace.

Glory be…

Antiphon
Lord our God, we praise the splendour of your name.

Reading *James 1:19-20, 26*

It is for us to be ready listeners, slow to speak our minds, slow to take offence; man's anger does not bear the fruit that is acceptable to God. If anyone deludes himself by thinking he is serving God, when he has not learned to control his tongue, the service he gives is in vain.

Short Responsory

℞ You are the Christ, the Son of the living God. Have mercy on us.
℣ You are seated at the right hand of the Father. Have mercy on us. ℞
Glory be… ℞

Benedictus/Magnificat Antiphon

Blessed be the Lord, for he has visited us and freed us.

Benedictus (if said in the morning) or **Magnificat** (if said in the evening) - see inside back cover for these prayers

Intercessions

Let us praise Christ, in whom is the fulness of grace and the Spirit of God.
℞ Lord, give us your Spirit.

We praise you, Lord, and we thank you for all your blessings.
℞ Lord, give us your Spirit.

Give us peace of mind and generosity of heart; grant us health and strength to do your will.
℞ Lord, give us your Spirit.

May your love be with us during the day; guide us in our work.
℞ Lord, give us your Spirit.

Be with all who have asked our prayers, and grant them all their needs.
℞ Lord, give us your Spirit.

Our Father…

Concluding prayer

Almighty Lord and God,
protect us by your power,
do not let us turn aside to any sin,
but let our every thought, word and deed
aim at doing what is pleasing in your
 sight.
Through Christ our Lord.
Amen.

The Pentecost by
unknown dutch enamel workers (c.1150-75)

Tuesday - Called to Share the Life of God

Introduction
O God, come to our aid. Lord, make haste to help us.

Glory be to the Father and to the Son and to the Holy Spirit, as it was in the beginning, is now, and ever shall be, world without end. Amen. (Alleluia)
omit Alleluias during Lent

Hymn
Come, Holy Spirit, live in us
With God the Father and the Son,
And grant us your abundant grace
To sanctify and make us one.

May mind and tongue made strong
  in love,
Your praise throughout the world
  proclaim,
And may that love within our hearts
Set fire to others with its flame.

Most blessed Trinity of love
For whom the heart of man was made,
To you be praise in timeless song,
And everlasting homage paid.

Antiphon
Blessed are they who live by the law of the Lord.

Psalmody   *Psalm 119(118)*
They are happy whose life is blameless,
who follow God's law!
They are happy who do his will,
seeking him with all their hearts,

who never do anything evil
but walk in his ways.
You have laid down your precepts
to be obeyed with care.

May my footsteps be firm
to obey your statutes.
Then I shall not be put to shame
as I heed your commands.

I will thank you with an upright heart
as I learn your decrees.
I will obey your statutes;
do not forsake me.

Glory be…

Antiphon
Blessed are they who live by the law of the Lord.

Reading   *Romans 13:11b, 12-13a*
You know what hour it is, how it is full time now for you to wake from sleep. The night is far gone, the day is at hand. Let us cast off the works of darkness and put on the armour of light; let us conduct ourselves becomingly as in the day.

Short Responsory
℟ My helper is my God; I will place all my trust in him.
℣ He is my refuge; he sets me free. ℟
Glory be… ℟

Benedictus/Magnificat Antiphon
Blessed be the Lord, for he has visited us and freed us.

Benedictus (if said in the morning)
or Magnificat (if said in the evening) -
see inside back cover for these prayers

Intercessions
As Christians called to share the life of God, let us praise the Lord Jesus, the high priest of our faith.
℟ You are our Saviour and our God.

Almighty King, you have baptised us, and made us a royal priesthood: may we offer you a constant sacrifice of praise.
℟ You are our Saviour and our God.

Help us to keep your commandments; so that through your Holy Spirit we may dwell in you, and you in us.
℟ You are our Saviour and our God.

Everlasting Wisdom, come to us: dwell in us and work in us today.
℟ You are our Saviour and our God.

Help us to be considerate and kind; grant that we may bring joy, not pain, to those we meet.
℟ You are our Saviour and our God.

Our Father…

Concluding prayer
True Light of the world, Lord Jesus Christ,
as you enlighten all for their salvation,
give us grace we pray,
to herald your coming
by preparing the ways of justice and peace.
Who live and reign with the Father and the Holy Spirit, God, for ever and ever.
Amen.

Angels at Mamre (also known as the Holy Trinity)
by Andrei Rublev (1360-1430)

Teach us, Lord Tuesday

Wednesday - O God Come to Our Aid

Introduction

O God, come to our aid. Lord, make haste
to help us.

Glory be to the Father and to the Son
and to the Holy Spirit, as it was in the
beginning, is now, and ever shall be,
world without end. Amen. (Alleluia)

omit Alleluias during Lent

Hymn

Now that the daylight fills the sky,
We lift our hearts to God on high,
That he, in all we do or say,
Would keep us free from harm today.

May he restrain our tongues from strife,
And shield from anger's din our life,
And guard with watchful care our eyes
From earth's absorbing vanities.

O may our inmost hearts be pure,
From thoughts of folly kept secure,
And pride of sinful flesh subdued
Through sparing use of daily food.

So we, when this day's work is o'er,
And shades of night return once more,
Our path of trial safely trod,
Shall give the glory to our God.

All praise to God the Father be,
All praise, eternal Son, to thee,
Whom with the Spirit we adore
Forever and forevermore.

Antiphon

In the day of my distress I sought the Lord
with outstretched arms.

Psalmody   *Psalm 55(54)*

O God, listen to my prayer,
do not hide from my pleading,
attend to me and reply;
with my cares, I cannot rest.

I tremble at the shouts of the foe,
at the cries of the wicked;
for they bring down evil upon me.
They assail me with fury.

My heart is stricken within me,
death's terror is on me,
trembling and fear fall upon me
and horror overwhelms me.

O that I had wings like a dove
to fly away and be at rest.
So I would escape far away
and take refuge in the desert.

I would hasten to find a shelter
from the raging wind,
from the destructive storm, O Lord,
and from their plotting tongues.

For I can see nothing
but violence and strife in the city.
Night and day they patrol
high on the city walls.

It is full of wickedness and evil;
it is full of sin.
Its streets are never free
from tyranny and deceit.

Glory be…

Daily Prayer **Teach us, Lord**

Antiphon
In the day of my distress I sought the Lord with outstretched arms.

Reading   *Isaiah 55:8-9*
My thoughts are not your thoughts,
my ways not your ways - it is the Lord
  who speaks.
Yes, the heavens are as high above the
  earth
as my ways are above your ways,
my thoughts above your thoughts.

Short Responsory
℟ Bend my heart to your will, O God.
℣ By your word, give me life. ℟
Glory be… ℟

Benedictus/Magnificat Antiphon
Do great things for us, O Lord, for you are mighty, and Holy is your name.

Benedictus (if said in the morning)
or Magnificat (if said in the evening) -
see inside back cover for these prayers

Intercessions
God is love: he who dwells in love dwells in God, and God in him. In Jesus Christ we see how God loves us. Let us renew our faith in his love:
℟ Lord Jesus, you gave yourself for us.

You are the sole master of the future: keep us from despair and the fear of what is to come.
℟ Lord Jesus, you gave yourself for us.

Love has no ambition to seek anything for itself: strengthen our will to give up selfishness today.
℟ Lord Jesus, you gave yourself for us.

May your love in us overcome all things: let there be no limit to our faith, our hope and our endurance.
℟ Lord Jesus, you gave yourself for us.

Our Father…

Concluding prayer
Lord God, in your wisdom you created us, by your providence you rule us:
penetrate us with your holy light,
so that we may always be faithful to you.
Through Christ our Lord.
Amen.

King David between Wisdom and Prophecy
in the Paris Psalter (10th century)

Thursday - Serve the Lord in Holiness

Introduction
O God, come to our aid. Lord, make haste to help us.

Glory be to the Father and to the Son and to the Holy Spirit, as it was in the beginning, is now, and ever shall be, world without end. Amen. (Alleluia)
                    omit Alleluias during Lent

Hymn
Lord God and Maker of all things,
Creation is upheld by you.
While all must change and know decay,
You are unchanging, always new.

You are man's solace and his shield,
His Rock secure on which to build,
You are the spirit's tranquil home,
In you alone is hope fulfilled.

To God the Father and the Son
And Holy Spirit render praise,
Blest Trinity, from age to age,
The strength of all our living days.

Antiphon
God of hosts, look down from heaven,
and come to visit this vine of yours.

Psalmody   *Psalm 80(79)*
O shepherd of Israel, hear us,
you who lead Joseph's flock,
shine forth from your cherubim throne
upon Ephraim, Benjamin, Manasseh.
O Lord, rouse up your might,
O Lord, come to our help.

God of hosts bring us back;
let your face shine on us and we shall be
  saved.

Lord God of hosts, how long
will you frown on your people's plea?
You have fed them with tears for their
  bread,
and abundance of tears for their drink.
You have made us the taunt of our
  neighbours,
our enemies laugh us to scorn.

God of hosts, bring us back;
let your face shine on us and we shall be
  saved.

You brought a vine our of Egypt;
to plant it you drove out the nations.
Before it you cleared the ground;
it took root and spread through the land.

The mountains were covered with its
  shadow,
the cedars of God with its boughs.
It stretched out its branches to the sea,
to the Great River it stretched out its
  shoots.

Glory be…

Antiphon
God of hosts, look down from heaven,
and come to visit this vine of yours.

Reading *Wisdom 19:20*
Yes, Lord, in every way you have made
your people great and glorious; you have
never distained them, but stood by them
always and everywhere.

Short Responsory
℟ I called with all my heart, Lord hear me.
℣ I will keep you commandments. ℟
Glory be… ℟

Benedictus/Magnificat Antiphon
Let us serve the Lord in holiness, and
he will deliver us from the hands of our
enemies.

Benedictus (if said in the morning)
or Magnificat (if said in the evening) -
see inside back cover for these prayers

Intercessions
We adore and praise our God who reigns
above the heavens. He is the Lord of
all things and before him all creation is
nothing.
℟ We adore you, our Lord and our God.

Lord be with us; move our hearts to seek
you and our wills to serve you.
℟ We adore you, our Lord and our God.

Deepen our awareness of your presence;
teach us reverence and love for all that
you have made.
℟ We adore you, our Lord and our God.

To know you is to love those you created:
let our lives and our work be of service to
our brothers and sisters.
℟ We adore you, our Lord and our God.

Our Father…

Concluding prayer
Almighty God,
you are all light,
in you there is no darkness.
Let your face shine upon us in all its
 radiance,
so that we might walk gladly in the way
 of your commandments.
Through Christ our Lord.
Amen.

Moses before Pharoah in the Syriac Bible of Paris

Friday - Remember Your Mercy, O Lord

Introduction

O God, come to our aid. Lord, make haste to help us.

Glory be to the Father and to the Son and to the Holy Spirit, as it was in the beginning, is now, and ever shall be, world without end. Amen. (Alleluia)

omit Alleluias during Lent

Hymn

I am the holy vine,
Which God my Father tends.
Each branch that yeilds no fruit
my Father cuts away.
Each fruitful branch
He prunes with care
To make it yield abundant fruit.

If you abide in me,
I will in you abide.
Each branch to yield its fruit
Must with the vine be one.
So you shall fail to yield your fruit.
If you are not with me one vine.

I am the fruitful vine,
And you my branches are.
He whoabides in me
I will in him abide.
So shall you yield
Much fruit, but none
If you remain apart from me.

Antiphon

A pure heart create for me, O God, put a steadfast spirit within me.

Psalmody *Psalm 51(50)*

Have mercy on me, God, in your kindness.
In your compassion blot out my offense.
O wash me more and more from my guilt
and cleanse me from my sin.

My offenses truly I know them;
my sin is always before me
Against you, you alone, have I sinned;
what is evil in your sight I have done.

Indeed you love truth in the heart;
then in the secret of my heart teach me wisdom.
O purify me, then I shall be clean;
O wash me, I shall be whiter than snow.

A pure heart create for me, O God,
put a steadfast spirit within me.
Do not cast me away from your presence,
nor deprive me of your holy spirit.

Give me again the joy of your help;
with a spirit of fervor sustain me,
that I may teach transgressors your ways
and sinners may return to you.

O rescue me, God, my helper,
and my tongue shall ring out your goodness.
O Lord, open my lips
and my mouth shall declare your praise.

For in sacrifice you take no delight,
burnt offering from me you would refuse,
my sacrifice, a contrite spirit,
a humbled, contrite heart you will not spurn.

Glory be…

Daily Prayer Teach us, Lord

Antiphon
A pure heart create for me, O God, put a steadfast spirit within me.

Reading   *Galatians 2:19b-20*
With Christ I hang upon the cross, and yet I am alive; or rather, not I; it is Christ that lives in me. True, I am living, here and now, this mortal life; but my real life is the faith I have in the Son of God, who loved me, and gave himself for me.

Short Responsory
℟ I call to the Lord, the Most High, for he has been my help.
℣ May he send from heaven and save me.
℟
Glory be… ℟

Benedictus/Magnificat Antiphon
Remember your mercy, O Lord; according to the promise you made to our fathers.

Benedictus (if said in the morning)
or Magnificat (if said in the evening) -
see inside back cover for these prayers

Intercessions
God's love for us was revealed when God sent into the world his only Son so that we might have life through him. We are able to love God because he loved us first. And so we pray:
℟ Lord help us to love you and one another

You look with compassion on the humble and contrite of heart; in your goodness, turn our hearts to you and help us to do what is right.
℟ Lord help us to love you and one another

Remember all those who put their hope in you while they lived: through the passion and death of your Son, grant them remission of all their sins.
℟ Lord help us to love you and one another

Our Father…

Concluding prayer
God of power and mercy,
you willed that Christ your Son should
  suffer for the salvation of all the world,
grant that your people may strive to offer
  themselves to you as a living sacrifice,
and may be filled with the fulness of
  your love.
Through Christ our Lord.
Amen.

Red Vineyards near Arles by
Vincent van Gogh (1888)

Saturday - As Christ Has Welcomed You

Introduction

O God, come to our aid. Lord, make haste to help us.

Glory be to the Father and to the Son and to the Holy Spirit, as it was in the beginning, is now, and ever shall be, world without end. Amen. (Alleluia)

omit Alleluias during Lent

Hymn

Eternal Father, loving God,
Who made us from the dust of earth,
Transform us by the Spirit's grace,
Give value to our little worth.

Prepare us for that day of days
When Christ from heaven will come with
 might
To call us out of dust again,
Our bodies glorified in light.

O Godhead, here untouched, unseen,
All things created bear your trace;
The seed of glory sown in man
Will flower when we see your face.

Antiphon

Your throne, O God, shall endure for ever.

Psalmody   *Psalm 45(44)*

My heart overflows with noble words.
To the king I must speak the song I have
 made,
my tongue as nimble as the pen of a scribe.

You are the fairest of the children of men
and graciousness is poured upon your lips:
because God has blessed you for evermore.

O mighty one, gird your sword upon
 your thigh;
in splendor and state, ride on in triumph
for the cause of truth and goodness
 and right.

Take aim with your bow in your dread
 right hand.
Your arrows are sharp, peoples fall
 beneath you.
The foes of the king fall down and
 lose heart.

Your throne, O God, shall endure for ever.
A scepter of justice is the scepter of your
 kingdom.
Your love is for justice; your hatred for evil.

Therefore God, your God, has anointed you
with the oil of gladness above other kings:
your robes are fragrant with aloes and myrrh.

From the ivory palace you are greeted
 with music.
The daughters of kings are among your
 loved ones.
On your right stands the queen in gold of
 Ophir.

Glory be…

Antiphon
Your throne, O God, shall endure for ever.

Reading
Romans 15:5-7

May the God of steadfastness and encouragement grant you to live in such harmony with one another, in accord with Christ Jesus, that together you may with one voice glorify the God and Father of our Lord Jesus Christ. Welcome one another, therefore, as Christ has welcomed you, for the glory of God.

Short Responsory
℟ I called to you, Lord, you are my refuge.
℣ You are all I have in the land of the living. ℟
Glory be… ℟

Benedictus/Magnificat Antiphon
Give your light, Lord, to those who sit in darkness and the shadow of death.

Benedictus (if said in the morning)
or Magnificat (if said in the evening) -
see inside back cover for these prayers

Intercessions
God's gift was not a spirit of timidity, but the Spirit of power, and love, and self-control. With complete confidence we pray:
℟ Father, send us your Spirit.

Praise be to God, in Christ you have given us every spiritual blessing
℟ Father, send us your Spirit.

Let our striving for your kingdom not fall short through selfishness and fear.
℟ Father, send us your Spirit.

Father, may your Spirit lead us out of solitude, may he lead us to open the eyes of the blind, to proclaim the Word of light, to reap together the harvest of life.
℟ Father, send us your Spirit.

Our Father…

Concluding prayer
Lord God,
living light of eternal love,
grant that always aglow with charity,
we may love you above all else
and our brethren for your sake,
with one and the selfsame love.
Through Christ our Lord.
Amen.

Detail from *Cathedra Petri* (1647-53) by Gian Lorenzo Bernini in St Peter's Basilica, Rome

Teach us, Lord Saturday

Supplementary Resources

Including: quotes for further reflection and prayers, St Dominic's Nine Ways of Prayer, a reflection on the Lord's Prayer based on Youcat, prayers for different times in life and prayers relating to the sacraments as well as some suggestions for further reading.

Image: Old Woman at Prayer by Nicholas Maes (c.1656)

Teach us, Lord

Quotes for further reflection

The function of prayer is not to influence God, but rather to change the nature of the one who prays.

Søren Kierkegaard (1813-1855)

The desire is thy prayers; and if thy desire is without ceasing, thy prayer will also be without ceasing. The continuance of your longing is the continuance of your prayer.

St Augustine of Hippo (354-430)

For prayer is nothing else than being on terms of friendship with God.

St Teresa of Ávila (1515-1582)

It is clear that he does not pray, who, far from uplifting himself to God, requires that God shall lower Himself to him, and who resorts to prayer not to stir the man in us to will what God wills, but only to persuade God to will what the man in us wills.

St Thomas Aquinas (1225-1274)

Prayer indeed is good, but while calling on the gods a man should himself lend a hand.

Hippocrates (BC460-377)

It is a common temptation of Satan to make us give up the reading of the Word and prayer when our enjoyment is gone; as if it were of no use to read the Scriptures when we do not enjoy them, and as if it were no use to pray when we have no spirit of prayer.

George Muller (1805-1898)

What most of all hinders heavenly consolation is that you are too slow in turning yourself to prayer.

Thomas à Kempis (1380-1471)

My longing for truth was a single prayer.

St Teresa Benedicta of the Cross - Edith Stein (1891-1942)

Prayer is not asking. Prayer is putting oneself in the hands of God, at his disposition, and listening to his voice in the depth of our hearts.

Blessed Mother Teresa of Calcutta (1910-1997)

A soul arms itself by prayer for all kinds of combat. In whatever state the soul may be, it ought to pray. A soul which is pure and beautiful must pray, or else it will lose its beauty; a soul which is striving after this purity must pray, or else it will never attain it; a soul which is newly converted must pray, or else it will fall again; a sinful soul, plunged in sins, must pray so that it might rise again. There is no soul which is not bound to pray, for every single grace comes to the soul through prayer.

St Faustina (1905-1938)

Prayer ought to be humble, fervent, resigned, persevering, and accompanied with great reverence. One should consider that he stands in the presence of God, and speaks with a Lord before whom the angels tremble from awe and fear.

St Mary Magdalen de Pazzi (1556-1607)

Prayer is an surge of the heart, it is a simple glance directed to heaven, it is a cry of gratitude and love in the midst of trail as well as joy; finally, it is something great, supernatural, which expands my soul and unites me to Jesus.

St Thérèse of Lisieux (1873-1897)

Prayer is the place of refuge for every worry, a foundation for cheerfulness, a source of constant happiness, a protection against sadness.

St John Chrysostom (347-407)

Prayer and work
Pray as though everything depended on God. Work as though everything depended on you.

St Augustine of Hippo (354-430)

Jacob did not cease to be a Saint because he had to attend to his flocks.

St Teresa of Ávila (1515-1582)

It is simply impossible to lead, without the aid of prayer, a virtuous life.

St John Chrysostom (347-407)

There are more tears shed over answered prayers than over unanswered prayers.

St Teresa of Ávila (1515-1582)

Virtues are formed by prayer. Prayer preserves temperance. Prayer suppresses anger. Prayer prevents emotions of pride and envy. Prayer draws into the soul the Holy Spirit, and raises man to Heaven.

St Ephraem of Syria (c.306-373)

Teach us, Lord

Let us all resign ourselves into his hands, and pray that in all things he may guide us to do his Holy Will ... When thoughts of this or that come I turn to him and say: 'Only what you will, my God. Use me as you will'.

St Mary of the Cross MacKillop (1842-1909)

He who prays most receives most.

St Alphonsus Maria de Liguori (1696-1787)

Types of prayer
Private prayer is like straw scattered here and there: If you set it on fire it makes a lot of little flames. But gather these straws into a bundle and light them, and you get a mighty fire, rising like a column into the sky; public prayer is like that.

St John Vianney (1786-1859)

We must meditate before, during and after everything we do. The prophet says: 'I will pray, and then I will understand.' This is the way we can easily overcome the countless difficulties we have to face day after day, which, after all, are part of our work. In meditation we find the strength to bring Christ to birth in ourselves and in others.

St Charles Borromeo (1538-1584)

We must speak to God as a friend speaks to his friend, servant to his master; now asking some favour, now acknowledging our faults, and communicating to him all that concerns us, our thoughts, our fears, our projects, our desires, and in all things seeking his counsel.

St Ignatius of Loyola (1491-1556)

During mental prayer, it is well, at times, to imagine that many insults and injuries are being heaped upon us, that misfortunes have befallen us, and then strive to train our heart to bear and forgive these things patiently, in imitation of our Saviour. This is the way to acquire a strong spirit.

St Philip Neri (1515-1595)

The prayer most pleasing to God is that made for others and particularly for the poor souls. Pray for them, if you want your prayers to bring high interest.

Blessed Anne Catherine Emmerich (1774-1824)

One must not think that a person who is suffering is not praying. He is offering up his sufferings to God, and many a time he is praying much more truly than one who goes away by himself and meditates his head off, and, if he has squeezed out a few tears, thinks that is prayer.

St Teresa of Ávila (1515-1582)

Teach us, Lord

Much more is accomplished by a single word of the Our Father said, now and then, from our heart, than by the whole prayer repeated many times in haste and without attention.

St Teresa of Ávila (1515-1582)

Without Prayer nothing good is done. God's works are done with our hands joined, and on our knees. Even when we run, we must remain spiritually kneeling before him.

St Luigi Orione (1872-1940)

Read some chapter of a devout book... It is very easy and most necessary, for just as you speak to God when at prayer, God speaks to you when you read.

St Vincent de Paul (1581-1660)

Are you making no progress in prayer? Then you need only offer God the prayers which the Saviour has poured out for us in the sacrament of the altar. Offer God his fervent love in reparation for your sluggishness.

St Margaret Mary Alacoque (1647-1690)

It often happens that we pray God to deliver us from some dangerous temptation, and yet God does not hear us but permits the temptation to continue troubling us. In such a case, let us understand that God permits even this for our greater good. When a soul in temptation recommends itself to God, and by His aid resists, O how it then advances in perfection.

St Alphonsus Maria de Liguori (1696-1787)

[The devil] dreads fasting, prayer, humility, and good works: he is not able even to stop my mouth who speak against him. The illusions of the devil soon vanish, especially if a man arms himself with the Sign of the Cross. The devils tremble at the Sign of the Cross of our Lord, by which he triumphed over and disarmed them.

St Anthony the Great (c.251-356)

Be always praying
Rejoice always, pray continually, give thanks in all circumstances; for this is God's will for you in Christ Jesus.

1 Thessalonians 5:16-18

We must pray without ceasing, in every occurrence and employment of our lives - that prayer which is rather a habit of lifting up the heart to God as in a constant communication with him.

St Elizabeth Ann Seton (1774-1821)

Teach us, Lord

Rather than set aside daily time for prayer, I pray constantly and spontaneously about everything I encounter on a daily basis. When someone shares something with me, I'll often simply say, 'let's pray about this right now.'

Thomas Kinkade (1958-2012)

We must pray without tiring, for the salvation of mankind does not depend on material success; nor on sciences that cloud the intellect. Neither does it depend on arms and human industries, but on Jesus alone.

St Frances Xavier Cabrini (1850-1917)

When I immersed myself in prayer and united myself with all the Masses that were being celebrated all over the world at that time, I implored God, for the sake of all these Holy Masses, to have mercy on the world and especially on poor sinners who were dying at that moment. At the same instant, I received an interior answer from God that a thousand souls had received grace through the prayerful mediation I had offered to God. We do not know the number of souls that is ours to save through our prayers and sacrifices; therefore, let us always pray for sinners.

St Faustina (1905-1938)

Prayer ought to be short and pure, unless it be prolonged by the inspiration of Divine grace.

St Benedict of Nursia (480-543)

Have confidence in prayer. It is the unfailing power which God has given us. By means of it you will obtain the salvation of the dear souls whom God has given you and all your loved ones. 'Ask and you shall receive,' Our Lord said. Be yourself with the good Lord.

St Peter Julian Eymard (1811-1868)

The Nine Ways of Prayer

The Nine Ways of Prayer of St Dominic is a treasured Dominican document on St Dominic's manner of praying. It was written by an anonymous author, probably at Bologna, between 1260 and 1288. Sister Cecilia of the Monastery of St Agnes at Bologna is the most likely source.

St Dominic knew that bodily gestures could powerfully dispose the soul to prayer. In this experience of bodily prayer, the soul in turn is lifted to God in an act of praise, thanksgiving, and supplication. These ways of prayer are a glimpse into the inner life of St Dominic and his intense love for God. We can make use of these in our private prayer (it is noted that St Dominic did not pray in these ways in public).

The first way (Inclinations): St Dominic humbled himself before the altar as if Christ, signified by the altar, were truly and personally present and not in symbol alone.

The second (Prostrations): St Dominic used to pray by throwing himself outstretched upon the ground, lying on his face. He would feel great remorse in his heart and call to mind those words of the Gospel: 'O God, be merciful to me, a sinner' [Luke 18:13].

The third (Penance): At the end of this prayer, St Dominic would rise from the ground and give himself the discipline with an iron chain, saying, 'Thy discipline has corrected me unto the end' [Psalm 17:36]. St Josemaria Escrivá recommends a type of mortification called 'the heroic minute'. It means getting up without hesitation and offering the day to the Lord: a supernatural reflection and... up! With this you will be well set up for the rest of the day.

The fourth (Genuflections): St Dominic would remain before the altar or in the chapter room with his gaze fixed on the Crucified One, looking upon Him with perfect attention. He genuflected frequently, again and again, like the leper of the gospel who said on bended knee: Lord, if Thou wilt, thou canst make me clean [Matthew. 8:2].

The fifth (Contemplation): St Dominic would sometimes remain before the altar, standing up without supporting himself or leaning upon anything. Often his hands would be extended before his breast in the manner of an open book; he would stand with great reverence and devotion as if reading in the very presence of God. Deep in prayer, he meditated upon the words of God.

Teach us, Lord

The sixth (Earnest Intercession): St Dominic, was also seen to pray standing erect with his hands and arms outstretched forcefully in the form of a cross.

The seventh (Supplication): While praying, he was often seen to reach towards heaven like an arrow straight upwards into the sky. He would stand with hands outstretched above his head and joined together, or at times slightly separated as if about to receive something from heaven. One would believe that he was receiving an increase of grace and in this rapture of spirit was asking God for the gifts of the Holy Spirit for the Order he had founded.

The eighth (Thoughtful Reading): St Dominic, had yet another manner of praying at once beautiful, devout, and pleasing, which he practiced after the canonical hours and the thanksgiving following meals. He quickly withdrew to some solitary place, to his cell or elsewhere, and recollected himself in the presence of God. He would sit quietly, and after the sign of the cross, begin to read from a book opened before him. His spirit would then be sweetly aroused as if he heard Our Lord speaking, as we are told in the psalms: I will hear what the Lord God will speak to me. [Psalm 84:9].

The ninth (Praying on a Journey): Lest any should think that the period of daily meditation were alone sufficient to the Christian soul (as though continual union with God throughout the day were not necessary), St Dominic taught us the ninth way of prayer. While travelling from one country to another, he delighted in giving himself completely to meditation, disposing for contemplation, and he would part from his companion. He would go on ahead or, more frequently, follow at some distance and, thus withdrawn, he would walk and pray. In his meditation he was inflamed and the fire of charity was enkindled. While he prayed it appeared as if he were brushing dust or bothersome flies from his face when instead he was repeatedly fortifing himself with the Sign of the Cross. It was thought that in praying in this way the saint obtained his extensive penetration of Sacred Scripture and profound understanding of the divine words, the power to preach so fervently and courageously, and that intimate acquaintance with the Holy Spirit by which he came to know the hidden things of God.

Our Father

'the most perfect prayer' (St Thomas Aquinas)

The following meditation is based on the section on the Lord's Prayer found in the Youth Catechism of the Catholic Church otherwise known as 'Youcat' (511-527). It can be used in private reflection, or as a responsorial prayer in your group or elsewhere in your parish.

Our Father ... *through baptism we are made adopted children of the Father*

who art in heaven ... *heaven denotes God's presence, not a place above the clouds*

hallowed be thy name ... *we honour God and treat his name as something holy*

thy kingdom come ... *we call for Christ to come again*

thy will be done ... *we pray not for our own wishes but God's plan for each one of us*

on earth as it is in heaven ... *just as Christ died on the Cross, we seek to do what is pleasing to God*

Give us this day our daily bread ... *we ask God to help us grow in trust that he will give us what we really need; both material and spiritual*

and forgive us our trespasses ... *we ask God to be merciful for we often turn away from him*

as we forgive those who trespass against us ... *we ask God to help us be more like Him - to forgive others*

and lead us not into temptation ... *we ask God to help us choose the good, to avoid the path that leads to sin*

but deliver us from evil ... *we ask God to keep us joined with Christ who died to save each one of us from all evils past, present and future*

Amen ... *from ancient times, Christians and Jews end their prayers with Amen... Yes, so be it!*

Teach us, Lord

The Beatitudes

'at the heart of Jesus' preaching' (CCC, 1716)

The following meditation is based on the section on the Beatitudes (Matthew 5:3-12) from Jesus' Sermon on the Mount (5:1 to 7:29) It can be used in private reflection, as an examination of conscience or as a prayer in your group or parish.

*Lord Jesus, you said, 'Blessed are the poor in spirit, for theirs is the kingdom of heaven.'
Keep me from being preoccupied with money and worldly goods, and with trying to increase them at the expense of justice.*

*Lord Jesus, you said, 'Blessed are the gentle, for they shall inherit the earth.'
Help me not to be ruthless with others, and to work to eliminate the discord and violence that exists in the world around me.*

*Lord Jesus, you said, 'Blessed are those who mourn, for they shall be comforted.'
Let me not be impatient under my own burdens and unconcerned about the burdens of others.*

*Lord Jesus, you said, 'Blessed are those who hunger and thirst for justice, for they shall be filled.'
Make me thirst for you, the fountain of all holiness, and actively spread your influence in my private life and in society.*

*Lord Jesus, you said, 'Blessed are the merciful, for they shall receive mercy.'
Grant that I may be quick to forgive and slow to condemn.*

*Lord Jesus, you said, 'Blessed are the clean of heart, for they shall see God.'
Free me from my senses and my evil desires, and fix my eyes on you.*

*Lord Jesus, you said, 'Blessed are the peacemakers, for they shall be called children of God.'
Aid me to make peace in my family, in my country, and in the world.*

*Lord Jesus, you said, 'Blessed are those who are persecuted for the sake of justice, for the kingdom of heaven in theirs.'
Make me willing to suffer for the sake of right rather than to practice injustice; and do not let me discriminate against my neighbours and oppress and persecute them.*

Teach us, Lord

Prayers ahead of the Sacraments

**For those approaching the
Sacrament of Reconciliation**
Lord Jesus,
you chose to be called the friend of sinners.
By your saving death and resurrection
free me from my sins.
May your peace take root in my heart
and bring forth a harvest
of love, holiness, and truth.

The Rite of Penance

**For those approaching the
Sacrament of Baptism**
Loving Father,
you enlighten us by Christ.
Help us to walk always as children of the light
and keep the flame of faith alive in our hearts.
When the Lord comes,
may we go out to meet him with all the saints
in the heavenly kingdom.

*Prayer which accompanies the presentation
of a lighted candle, The Rite of Baptism, adapted*

**For those approaching the
Sacrament of Confirmation**
In baptism,
God our Father gave the new birth of
eternal life to his sons and daughters.
Let us pray to our Father that he
will pour out the Holy Spirit
to strengthen us, his sons and daughters,
with his gifts and anoint us to be more like
Christ, the Son of God.
Amen.

*Laying on of hands from
the Rite of Confirmation, adapted*

**We pray for others celebrating the
Sacrament of Reconciliation**
May the grace of the Holy Spirit
fill our hearts with light,
that we may confess our sins with loving trust
and come to know that God is merciful.

The Rite of Penance, adapted

**We pray for others celebrating the
Sacrament of Baptism**
Almighty and eternal God,
you bless your Church with new members.
Deepen the faith and understanding of
those candidates chosen for baptism.
Give them a new birth in your living waters
and make them members of your family.
We ask this through Christ our Lord.

*Good Friday, Prayers of Intercession,
For Those Preparing for Baptism*

**We pray for others celebrating the
Sacrament of Confirmation**
All-powerful God,
Father of our Lord Jesus Christ,
by water and the Holy Spirit
you freed your sons and daughters from sin
and gave them new life.
Send your Holy Spirit upon them
be their Helper and Guide.
Give them the spirit of wisdom
and understanding,
the spirit of right judgment and courage,
the spirit of knowledge and reverence.
Fill them with the spirit of wonder and awe
in your presence.
We ask this through Christ our Lord.

Prayer from the Rite of Confirmation

Teach us, Lord

Prayer for those approaching the Sacrament of the Eucharist and we pray for others celebrating the same
Lord, look upon this sacrifice
which you have given to your Church;
and by your Holy Spirit,
gather all who share this one bread
and one cup
into the one Body of Christ,
a living sacrifice of praise.

From Eucharistic Prayer IV (1974 Missal)

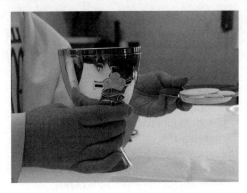

Prayers for different times and uses

Rite of Blessing of a Child in the Womb

Highlighted in an intervention at the recent Synod on the New Evangelisation, the Holy Sea has approved a 'Rite for the Blessing of a Child in the Womb' that was crafted by the US Conference of Catholic Bishops to support expectant parents awaiting the birth of their child, to encourage parish prayers for - and recognition of - the precious gift of the child in the womb, and to foster respect for human life within society. It may be offered within the context of the Mass as well as outside of Mass.

God, author of all life,
bless, we pray, this unborn child;
give constant protection
and grant a healthy birth
that is the sign of our rebirth one day
into the eternal rejoicing of heaven.

excerpt from the Prayer of Blessing

A short prayer for everyday

Lord Jesus Christ, Son of the living God, have mercy on me, a sinner.

The Jesus Prayer

For a parent

I dedicate my child to you, Lord. I recognise that he[she] is always in your care.

Help me as a parent, Lord, with my weaknesses and imperfections. Give me strength and godly wisdom to raise this child after your Holy Word. Please supply what I lack. Keep my child walking on the path that leads to eternal life. Help him to overcome the temptations in this world and the sin that would so easily entangle him.

Dear God, send your Holy Spirit daily to lead and guide him. Ever assist him to grow in wisdom and stature, in grace and knowledge, in kindness, compassion and love. May he serve you faithfully with his whole heart devoted to you. May he discover the joy of your presence through daily relationship with your Son, Jesus.

Help me never to hold on too tightly to this child, nor neglect my responsiblities before you as a parent. Lord, let my committment to raise this child for the glory of your name cause his life to forever testify of your faithfulness.

A morning offering

O Jesus, through the Immaculate Heart of Mary,
I offer you my prayers, works, joys, sufferings of this day,
in union with the Holy Sacrifice of the Mass throughout the world.
I offer them for all the intentions of your Sacred Heart;
the salvation of souls, the reparation for sin, the reunion of all Christians;
I offer them for the intentions of our bishops and of all members of the Apostleship of Prayer,
and in particular for those recommended by the Holy Father (i.e., the Pope) this month.
Amen.

Morning offering to the Sacred Heart of Jesus

A second morning prayer

Father in heaven
I give you today
all that I think and do, and say.
And I offer it up
with all that was done
by Jesus Christ your only Son.
Amen.

A Night prayer

After making a short review of the day, briefly recalling with gratitude the good things that have happened, and repenting in sincere sorrow the sins you have committed, say this prayer.

Eternal Father,
I desire to rest in Thy Heart this night.
I make the intention of offering to Thee every beat of my heart,
joining to them as many acts of love and desire.
I pray that even while I am asleep,
I will bring back to Thee souls that offend Thee.
I ask forgiveness for the whole world,
especially for those who know Thee and yet sin.
I offer to Thee my every breath and heartbeat as a prayer of reparation.
Amen.

A short prayer to the Holy Spirit

Come Holy Spirit,
fill the hearts of your faithful
and kindle in them the fire of your love.
Send forth your Spirit,
and they shall be created.
And you shall renew the face of the earth.

The Agony in the Garden by El Greco (c.1608)

Teach us, Lord

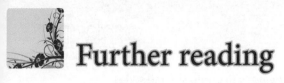

Further reading

John Bartunek (2008) *The Better Part: A Christ-Centered Resource for Personal Prayer*, Circle Press

Michael Buckley (2013) *The Catholic Prayer Book*, St Anthony Messenger Press

Stan Fortuna C.E.R. (2004) *U Got 2 Pray*, Our Sunday Visitor

YOUCAT Prayer Book (2013) Catholic Truth Society

Bl John Paul II (1998) *Prayers and Devotions: 365 Daily Meditations*, Penguin Books

St Teresa of Ávila (2007) *The Interior Castle,* Ave Maria Press

Jeffrey Pinyan (2009) *Praying the Mass*, CreateSpace

Peter Kreeft (2000) *Prayer for Beginners*, Ignatius Press

Bl Mother Teresa (2009) *Everything Starts from Prayer,* White Cloud Press

Benedict XVI (2013) *A School of Prayer: The Saints Show us How to Pray*, Ignatius Press [a collection of the texts from general audiences, also available on www.vatican.va]

Christopher Hayden (2001) *Praying the Scriptures: A Practical Introduction to Lectio Divina*, St Pauls Publishing

Michael Cleary (2011) *The Jesus Prayer Rosary: Bible Meditations for Praying with Beads*, Canterbury Press

Maite Roche (2007) *First Prayers for Little Children*, Catholic Truth Society

Let us pray (2009) WRCDT [online at http://issuu.com/exploringfaith/docs/let_us_pray]

There are many references to prayer among papal documents, for example:
Bl John Paul II (2002) *Rosarium Virginis Mariae*; (2001) *Novo Millennio Ineunte*, 32-34; (1981) *Familiaris Consortio*, 59-62 and Benedict XVI (2007) *Spe Salvi*, 32

Teach us, Lord

Some other booklets in the *exploring faith* group sharing series

Hail Mary, Full of Grace (published autumn 2010)

Six group sessions for faith-sharing which explore what the Scriptures and the Church say about Mary - the immaculately conceived, sinless, ever-virgin, mother of Christ, assumed into heaven.

978-0-9563514-4-9   £1.50 where sold

Sparks of Light (published Lent 2012)

Six group sessions for faith-sharing which explore, through the lives of four twentieth-century saints, the universal call to holiness and virtue.

978-0-9570793-2-8   £1.50 where sold

Radiating Christ (published autumn 2012)

Six group sessions for faith-sharing which explore, the call to spread the Good News of Jesus Christ and the idea of faith in today's world.

978-0-9570793-3-5   £1.50 where sold

Amazing Grace (published Lent 2013)

Six group sessions for faith-sharing exploring the call to continuing conversion and the mercy and love shown by God to his children.

978-0-9570793-6-6   £1.50 where sold

Each of the previous resources in the *exploring faith* series can be downloaded and viewed by visiting the Diocese of Westminster's website or can be purchased from our bookstore. If you have a QR reader simply scan the code (*right*) and you will be directed to the relevant webpage (www.rcdow.org.uk/bookstore).

Teach us, Lord